P9-BIM-511

Paint the town : images
in art, Los Altos and Lo
c2000.
33305015202199
cu   05/28/19

PAINT THE TOWN™

Images in Art
Los Altos and Los Altos Hills—The Last Year Of The 20th Century

❖ ❖ ❖ ❖ ❖ ❖ ❖ ❖ ❖ ❖ ❖

"It is art that makes life . . . I know of no substitute
whatever for the force and beauty of its process."
Henry James 1915

❖ ❖ ❖ ❖ ❖ ❖ ❖ ❖ ❖ ❖ ❖

COMPILED BY PAUL & LIZ NYBERG

SANTA CLARA COUNTY LIBRARY

3 3305 01520 2199

PAINT THE TOWN

All rights reserved. No part of this publication may be reproduced
or transmitted in any form or by any means, electronic or mechanical,
including photocopying, recording, or any information storage
and retrieval system, without permission in writing from the publisher.

Library of Congress Number: 00-192401
ISBN 0-9634623-2-6
Copyright 2000 by Select Communications, Inc.
Published by Select Books,
Division of Select Communications, Inc.
138 Main Street
Los Altos CA 94022

Printed in the USA
Print Innovations, Inc., Sunnyvale CA 94089
First Edition

"All books are divisible into two classes: the books of the hour, and the books of all time."
John Ruskin, 1865

Preface

In the summer of 1999 and in early 2000, artists from the greater Los Altos, California area were invited to "paint the town," to capture with paint or ink what Los Altos and Los Altos Hills looked like the last year of the 20th century. This book is a collection of their work, a "book for all time" since it provides a snap shot of local history within its pages. The buildings and scenes included here were chosen by the individual artists from over 400 commercial and public buildings in Los Altos and Los Altos Hills. While this may be a book for all time, the community's look changes with regularity. Between the time these paintings were completed and this book went to press, ten buildings in the Village of Los Altos changed their faces as businesses ceased operation or changed ownership.

Acknowledgements

Special appreciation is due the ad hoc "Paint The Town" Committee who helped recruit the artists and organize the painting efforts in 1999. The committee included Shannon Elam, Katherine Frey and Jeane Kluga. Gail Vanderberg was invaluable in her efforts coordinating the scheduling and maintaining an exhaustive database of participants. Monique Schoenfeld produced the color scans and color separations for all pages. The effort was supported by the *Los Altos Town Crier*, for more than 50 years the community voice of Los Altos.

Financial Underwriters

This publication was created for the Los Altos Cultural Association to be a gift to the community as a fund-raiser for nonprofit organizations. Initial grants to help fund the direct costs for printing and production were generously underwritten by the **David and Lucile Packard Foundation** and the **Steven and Michele Kirsch Foundation.** Additional donors are listed on the dust jacket.

Paul & Liz Nyberg
Los Altos, California, 2000 A.D.

Our Village

". . . the loveliest village of the plain,
Where health and plenty cheered the laboring swain,
Where smiling spring its earliest visit paid,
And parting summer's lingering blooms delayed."
Oliver Goldsmith 1770

DENISE NATANSON-MARCUS • DEMARTINI ORCHARD • 66 NORTH SAN ANTONIO ROAD • *OIL ON CANVAS* • *18" x 36"*

*First established early in the 20th Century, this roadside fruit and vegetable stand
continues to prosper as a business and as a community landmark.*

LARRAINE HUGHES • OFFICE BUILDING • 40 MAIN STREET • *WATERCOLOR ON PAPER* • *16" x 20"*

Picturesque location for real estate, legal and accounting offices.

"From every house the neighbours met,
The streets were fill'd with joyful sound."
Alfred Tennyson 1850

JEANE KLUGA • MUSICIANS IN THE PLAZA • MAIN & STATE STREETS • *ACRYLIC ON CANVAS* • *22" x 28"*

JIM M'GUINNESS • MAIN STREET AT EDITH AVENUE • *LATEX ON STUCCO* • *10 FEET X 28 FEET*

*A community paint-by-the-number mural designed by Jim M'Guinness as a fund raiser
for the purchase of the Olympic Wannabes sculpture.*

JEAN FRANCO • CHRISTIAN SCIENCE LIBRARY • 60 MAIN STREET • *WATERCOLOR ON WATERCOLOR PAPER* • *14" x 20"*

NANCY & NORMAN BETTINI • MAIN STREET OFFICES • 111 MAIN STREET • *OIL ON CANVAS* • *15" x 30"*

Home to many retail and business offices over the years including the Los Altos Village Association.

JEAN WARREN • CITIBANK & PLAZA CLOCK • MAIN & STATE STREETS • *WATERCOLOR ON D'ARCHES PAPER • 22" X 30"*

Remodeled in 1993, the bank building is a backdrop for the Community Plaza
which was created the same year with funds provided by the Los Altos Rotary Club.

To everything there is a season, and
A time to every purpose under the heaven:
A time to be born, and a time to die;
A time to plant, and a time to pluck up;
A time to kill, and a time to heal;
A time to break down, and a time to build up;
A time to weep, and a time to laugh;
A time to mourn, and a time to dance;
A time to get, and a time to lose;
A time to keep, and a time to cast away
A time to rend, and a time to sew;
A time to keep silence, and a time to speak;
To everything there is a season.
Ecclesiastes 3.

Clock donated in 1993 in memory of Denny Spangler--
City Council member and longtime community
volunteer--by his wife, Louise Spangler,
and other contributors.

DIANE BRAUCH • COMMUNITY PLAZA CLOCK • STATE & MAIN STREETS • CHARCOAL ON PAPER • 16" x 20"

MARGE ARNOLD • SHOKO'S OF LOS ALTOS & COOKIE CAFE • 135 MAIN STREET • *WATERCOLOR* • *15" x 24"*

"Speak the speech, I pray you,
as I pronounced it to you,
trippingly on the tongue;
but if you mouth it,
as many of your players do,
I had as lief the town crier spoke my
lines."
William Shakespeare (Hamlet)

- **KATHY SHARPE**
- CHRISTMAS DAY ON MAIN STREET
- VIEWED FROM THE TOWN CRIER BUILDING
- *WATERCOLOR • 30" X 22"*

"The newspaper is of necessity something of a monopoly, and its first duty is to shun the temptations of monopoly. Its primary office is the gathering of news. At the peril of its soul it must see that the supply is not tainted. Neither in what it gives, nor in what it does not give, nor in the mode of presentation, must the unclouded face of truth suffer wrong. Comment is free, but facts are sacred."
C.P. Scott 1926

PATRICIA HOWARD •
LOS ALTOS TOWN CRIER •
138 MAIN STREET •
OIL ON CANVAS • 20" X 15" •

JUDI KEYANI • MARJOLAINE FRENCH PASTERIES • 134 MAIN STREET • *PASTEL ON PAPER* • *15" X 25"*

Remodeled in 1995 for the permanent home of the 50 year old Los Altos Town Crier, the first floor was once occupied by retail stores, a beauty shop and a real estate office; the second floor was the first offices of Systan, Inc. in the late sixties.

DOROTHY MURPHY • ITALIAN DELICATESSEN • 139 MAIN STREET • *WATERCOLOR* • *16" x 20"*

JIM M'GUINNESS • DAVINO FLORIST • 149 MAIN STREET • *WATERCOLOR & INK ON PAPER* • *14" x 11"*

DENISE NATANSON-MARCUS • LOS ALTOS BAR & GRILL • 169 MAIN STREET • *OIL ON CANVAS* • *24" x 30"*

Center of night life in downtown Los Altos for over three decades.

DENISE NATANSON-MARCUS • SANWA BANK • 176 MAIN STREET • *OIL ON CANVAS* • *18" x 24"*

Built as a bank in the 1940s, the building has seen numerous bank names on its marquee.

KATHY SHARPE • KAHN'S CORNER PHARMACY • THIRD & MAIN STEETS • *WATERCOLOR* • 12" x 17"

This Main Street landmark was the first commercial building designed by distinquished local architect, Goody Steinberg

"The purest and most thoughtful minds are those which love colour the most."
John Ruskin 1859

JAN MEYER • COVER STORY • 216 MAIN STREET • *OIL ON CANVAS* • *20" x 20"*

The first firehouse for the growing village was established here in early 1900.

BERNI JAHNKE • STARBUCKS COFFEE • 296 MAIN STREET • *WATERCOLOR* • *16" x 20"*

A popular hangout for coffee drinkers in the last years of the 20th century, this landmark building on Main Street has served as a real estate office, a jewelry store and a women's clothing store.

*"For the bread that you eat
and the biscuits you nibble . . .
they are brought to you daily by us . . ."*
Rudyard Kipling 1898

CARLA BJORK • LE BOULANGER • 301 MAIN STREET • *OIL ON CANVAS* • *20" x 16"*

This corner was occupied by Los Altos Pharmacy for many years in the mid-1900s.

MARGE ARNOLD • MAIN STEET LOOKING SOUTH FROM SECOND STREET • *WATERCOLOR ON 300 LB. HOT PRESS PAPER • 11" X 15"*

JAYNE SHIELDS • BAYVIEW BANK • 300 MAIN STREET • *WATERCOLOR • 15" x 20"*

Oldest building on Main Street was built by Paul Shoup for commercial and office use in 1908.
The first grammar school met upstairs. For many years Gene Tarbell Women's Wear was located downstairs.

WILL MALLER • MAC'S AMERICAN GRILL • 325 MAIN STREET • *OIL ON CANVAS* • *16" x 22"*

Oldest restaurant on Main Street, originally Mac's Tea Room, closed its doors in the spring of 2000.

PATRICIA HOWARD • AL'S BARBER SHOP • 368 MAIN STREET • *WATERCOLOR* • *11" x 14"*

Built in 1923, served as a barber shop continuously for 76 years until 1999 when the building was remodeled.

JEAN WARREN • COPELAND BUILDING • 397 MAIN STREET • *WATERCOLOR ON D'ARCHES PAPER* • *22" X 30"*

*This historic building was once occupied by doctors on the second floor; the street level was
at one time a pharmacy, a silent movie theatre and the first post office.*

LARRAINE HUGHES • HOME CONSIGNMENT CENTER • 400 MAIN STREET • *WATERCOLOR ON PAPER* • *16" x 20"*

First occupied by Gordon's Market, later was one of the first Kentucky Fried Chicken franchises in the West.

Floy Zittin • Village Chevron • 401 Main Street • *Watercolor On Bristol Board* • *15" x 22"*

*"The doctor can bury his mistakes,
but the architect can only
advise his client to plant vines."
Frank Lloyd Wright 1950*

- **PATRICIA HOWARD**
- FLOWERS IN THE PLAZA
- STATE AND MAIN STREETS
- *WATERCOLOR • 20" x 16"*

CAROLYN HOFSTETTER • COSTUME BANK • 169 STATE STREET • *OIL ON CANVAS* • *18" x 24"*

For many years a Los Altos fire station.

MILLIE GALLO • LUCKY CHINESE RESTAURANT • 140 STATE STREET • *WATERCOLOR ON PAPER* • *10" x 15"*

JEANE KLUGA • DESIGN & INTERIORS • 170 STATE STREET • *WATERCOLOR* • *16" x 20"*

Historic site of a large downtown grocery, Purity Market.

JOYCE SAVRE • LINDEN TREE CHILDREN'S RECORDS & BOOKS • 170 STATE STREET • *WATERCOLOR ON PAPER* • *22" x 30"*

Previously was a sportswear shop.

DIANE BERGH • TOUR EIFFEL RESTAURANT • 200 STATE STREET • *WATERCOLOR* • *14" x 18"*

Oldtimers remember this location as the "Scotch Box," a wine and spirits store.

JIM M'GUINNESS • HEINTZELMAN'S BOOKSTORE • 205 MAIN STREET • *WATERCOLOR & INK ON PAPER • 11" x 16"*

Two noted local artists provide their interpretation of this popular bookshop on State Street.

JAN MEYER • HEINTZELMAN'S BOOKSTORE • 205 MAIN STREET • *OIL ON CANVAS* • *20" x 20"*

One time home to the Los Altos Post Office.

KATHY SHARPE • LIN'S TOY CUPBOARD • 237 STATE STREET • *OIL ON CANVAS* • *22" x 28"*

KEVIN KASIK •
CHARLEY'S RESTAURANT •
244 STATE STREET •
ACRYLIC ON PANEL •
19" x 13" •

DONNA KEIFFER • BASKIN-ROBBINS • 264 STATE STREET • *OIL • 14" x 18"*

There has always been an ice cream store here.

MARGE ARNOLD • CRANBERRY SCOOP • 295 STATE STREET • *Watercolor on 300 lb. hot press paper* • *11" x 15"*

First built in the 1950s as a real estate office, was also the location of a pharmacy for 20 years.

A few days after this painting was completed, Cottage Collectibles ceased operation.

Zoe Joyce Orth
- Cottage Collectibles
- 276 State Street
- *Oil On Canvas*
- *20" x 16"*

LILLIAN BALLIET • COURTYARD CAFE • 301 STATE STREET • *WATERCOLOR ON PAPER* • *20" x 28"*

Originally a floor coverings store, later a coffee shop, a Japanese restaurant
and shortly after this painting was completed became Ay Ay Ay.

ROBYN CRUMBY • VIEWPOINTS GALLERY • 315 STATE SREEET • *WATERCOLOR ON PAPER* • *10" X 13"*

Before becoming an art gallery, served as a real estate office and a dress shop.

DOROTHY MURPHY • PATT'S GREENHOUSE • 366 STATE STREET • *WATERCOLOR* • *16" x 20"*

MILLIE GALLO • FAST FRAME • 371 STATE STREET • *WATERCOLOR ON PAPER • 10" x 14"*

FLOY ZITTIN • PEET'S COFFEE & TEA • 367 STATE STREET • *WATERCOLOR ON BRISTOL BOARD* • *15" x 22"*

JEAN FRANCO • COLDWELL BANKER • 110 FIRST STREET • *WATERCOLOR ON WATERCOLOR PAPER* • *14" x 20"*

Newly constructed in the early 1990s as a real estate office.

MILLICENT BISHOP • CASA DE BELLE COSE • 145 FIRST STREET •*WATERCOLOR* • *19" x 28"*

A one-time private residence on First Street became an antique store.

KATHY SHARPE • PRIMA STRADA • 127 FIRST STREET • *OIL ON LINEN* • *22" X 30"*

Originally a glass company, the site was remodeled into Prima Strada,
which in late 1999 became Adobe Creek Restaurant.

PATRICIA HOWARD • MARIA'S ANTIQUES OF LOS ALTOS • 288 FIRST STREET • *WATERCOLOR* • *16" x 20"*

This historic Southern Pacific railway station was built in 1908 and served until 1964 when the tracks were replaced by Foothill Expressway. A well preserved landmark, the building has since served as a restaurant and a bank.

Retired Caboose @ the former
Los Altos Train Station
now Maria's Antiques

ROBERT F. DEMANGE • OLD CABOOSE AT TRAIN STATION • 288 FIRST STREET •*WATERCOLOR ON ARCHES PAPER* • *15" x 21"*

Now at rest at the site of the historic Southern Pacific railroad station, which put Los Altos on the map in 1908.

FERENC BESZE • SILAN RESTAURANT • 376 FIRST STREET • *WATERCOLOR ON PAPER* • *15" x 22"*

For decades the location was occupied by the Black Forest Inn which had hand-painted murals of mountain scenes.

FLOY ZITTIN • LOS ALTOS HARDWARE • 441 FIRST STREET • *WATERCOLOR ON BRISTOL BOARD • 10" x 14"*

A corner of the community made famous for decades by Clint's Ice Cream. The building behind the flag was Bullock's Cleaners.

A long history as a restaurant--at one time a radio show broadcast on a Palo Alto radio station originated from here.

JOHN BURTON •
VILLAGE PANTRY •
184 SECOND STREET •
OIL ON CANVAS •
40" X 30" •

BERNI JAHNKE • MALTBY'S RESTAURANT • 101 NORTH PLAZA • *WATERCOLOR* • *16" x 20"*

"It's good food and not fine words that keep me alive." - Moliere 1672

LEONARD LEVING • BANDERA RESTAURANT • 233 THIRD STREET • *WATERCOLOR ON PAPER* • *14" x 28"*

This site started life as Gene Tarbell Women's Wear, followed by a pizza parlor, antique store and a large stationery store.

300 Second Street

JAN BAZA • PACKARD FOUNDATION • 300 SECOND STREET • *WATERCOLOR* • *14" x 20"*

"Architecture in general is frozen music." Friedrich Von Schelling 1809

Our Community

I'd rather be first in a village than second in Rome.
Julius Caesar 44 BC

❖ ❖ ❖ ❖ ❖ ❖ ❖ ❖ ❖ ❖ ❖ ❖ ❖ ❖

"There never was a good war,
or a bad peace."
Benjamin Franklin 1783

Cradle of Liberty, a veterans' memorial created
by Los Altan R.J. Truman, was dedicated in
Shoup Park July 4, 1998 at a ceremony attended
by over three thousand persons.

- **PATRICIA HOWARD**
- CRADLE OF LIBERTY
- SHOUP PARK
- *OIL ON CANVAS • 20" x 16"*

DOROTHY MURPHY • LOS ALTOS CHAMBER OF COMMERCE • 321 UNIVERSITY AVENUE • *WATERCOLOR ON PAPER* • *16" x 20"*

Designed by local architect Goody Steinberg, this rustic contemporary "home" for the chamber was dedicated in 1961.

ADRIENNE GILLESPIE • BANK OF LOS ALTOS, MAIN OFFICE • 4546 EL CAMINO REAL • *OIL ON CANVAS* • *16" x 20"*

DENISE NATANSON-MARCUS • ARMADILLO WILLY'S BBQ & CAFE • 1031 NORTH SAN ANTONIO ROAD • *OIL ON CANVAS* • *16" x 20"*

JENNY NEWBERRY • SAN ANTONIO CLUB • SAN ANTONIO ROAD • *OIL ON CANVAS* • *16" x 20"*

Early literary and women's club house, and in recent years a pre-school, has never been a residence.

CONNIE F. ABBOTT • HISTORY HOUSE • LOS ALTOS CIVIC CENTER • *ACRYLIC ON CANVAS* • *16" x 20"*

Built by J. Gilbert Smith in 1905, the home was opened as a museum in 1977. The ten acre apricot orchard
surrounding the home was purchased by the city in 1954 for the civic center site.

KAREN MELBY • OLYMPIC WANNABES • CONNER PARK • *WATERCOLOR • 10" x 14"*

Purchased with funds raised by the Los Altos Cultural Association, this new landmark found its home in the new park across San Antonio Road from the Civic Center in early 2000.

DIANE BERGH • WATER TOWER IN SPRING • LOS ALTOS HISTORY MUSEUM • *WATERCOLOR ON PAPER* • *10" x 14"*

CONNIE F. ABBOT • WATER TANK TOWER • LOS ALTOS HISTORY MUSEUM • *ACRYLIC ON CANVAS • 16" x 20"*

DIANE BERGH • ORCHARDS IN SPRINGTIME • LOS ALTOS HISTORY MUSEUM • *WATERCOLOR ON PAPER* • *10" x 14"*

". . . poems are made by fools like me, but only God can make a tree."
Joyce Kilmer 1914

BETSY REEVES • LOS ALTOS POLICE STATION • 1 NORTH SAN ANTONIO ROAD • *WATERCOLOR* • *16" x 20"*

DOROTHY MURPHY • LOS ALTOS CITY HALL • 1 NORTH SAN ANTONIO ROAD • *WATERCOLOR ON PAPER* • *15" x 21"*

"Die politik ist die lehre von moglichen." Prince Bismarck 1867

" . . . a circulating library in a town is as an evergreen tree . . . those who are so fond of handling the leaves, will long for the fruit at last."
Richard Brinsley Sheridan 1777

JUDI KEYANI • LOS ALTOS PUBLIC LIBRARY • 13 SOUTH SAN ANTONIO ROAD • *PASTEL ON PAPER* • *18" x 21"*

The highest per capita circulation library in Santa Clara County, the building originally constructed in 1965 was modernized and enlarged in the mid-1990s.

WILL MALLER • LOS ALTOS NURSERY • 245 HAWTHORNE • *OIL ON CANVAS* • *16" x 20"*

Owned and operated by the Furuichi family for three generations.

ROBERT C. SCHICK • LOS ALTOS NURSERY TANK HOUSE • 245 HAWTHORNE • *OIL ON LINEN* • *20" x 30"*

After nearly a century of service and architectural character, the tank house was torn down in early 2000 to make way for new homes.

KEVIN KASIK • THE ECHO • 1579 MIRAMONTE AVENUE • *OIL ON CANVAS* • *16" x 20"*

KIM DOMINO • TOM'S ICE CREAM DEPOT • 991 FREMONT AVENUE • *GOUACHE WATERCOLOR* • *10" x 14"*

ROBERT C. SCHICK • STEVE ALBIN PICTURE FRAMING • RANCHO SHOPPING CENTER • *OIL ON LINEN* • *20" x 24"*

MILLICENT BISHOP • POST OFFICE AND GIFT SHOP • RANCHO SHOPPPING CENTER • *WATERCOLOR* • *14" x 18"*

*"Prayer was not our last resort.
It was our first response."
Chuck Geschke, explaining
his kidnapping ordeal in 1995.*

DEBORAH MENDIVIL •
ST. NICHOLAS CATHOLIC CHURCH •
473 LINCOLN AVENUE •
ACRYLICS •
24" X 20" •

*"If you don't know
where to turn,
when you don't know
where to turn,
then you have nothing."
Alan Simpson
Celebrity Forum, 2000*

MAUREEN KEENAN BRAUN • EL RETIRO SAN INIGO • 300 MANRESA WAY • *ACRYLIC ON CANVAS* • *30" x 30"*

This Catholic-owned retreat center welcomes groups of all kinds for educational and inspirational meetings.

LARRAINE HUGHES • FOOTHILLS CONGREGATIONAL CHURCH • 461 ORANGE AVENUE • *WATERCOLOR ON PAPER* • *12" x 16"*

*Originally built by the parishioners of Christ Episcopal Church, the buildings
have sheltered Foothills Congregational worshippers since the early 1960s.*

MARGE ARNOLD • ST. NICHOLAS CATHOLIC CHURCH • *WATERCOLOR ON PAPER* • *11" x 15"*

"I will lift mine eyes to the hills,
from whence cometh my help.
My help cometh from the Lord."
Psalms 121:1-2

DOROTHY MURPHY • CHRIST EPISCOPAL CHURCH • 1040 BORDER ROAD • *WATERCOLOR* • *22 x 15*

KIM DOMINO • OAK ELEMENTARY SCHOOL • 1501 OAK AVENUE • *GOUCHE WATERCOLOR* • *10" x 14"*

LARRAINE HUGHES • PILGRIM HAVEN GAZEBO • 373 PINE LANE • *WATERCOLOR ON PAPER* • *17" x 23"*

Built in 1999 on the site where an ancient oak had recently fallen.

CARLA BJORK • REDWOOD GROVE NATURE CENTER • *OIL ON CANVAS* • *16" x 20"*

BONNIE HICKS • HORSE SCULPTURE • LINCOLN PARK • *OIL ON BOARD* • *12" x 16"*

"Brawn" by artist Jabe Jackson was one of many "sculptures on loan" managed by the Los Altos Arts Committee.

JEAN STRUTHERS • WESTWIND BARN • 27210 ALTAMONT ROAD LAH • *OIL ON CANVAS* • *20" x 24"*

LARRAINE HUGHES • HIDDEN VILLA WHITE HOUSE • 26870 MOODY ROAD LAH • *WATERCOLOR ON PAPER* • *16" x 20"*

*Shipped around the Horn to Los Altos Hills in 1840, the structure was reportedly
a stage coach stop on the route from Mountain View to Pescadero near the coast.*

ADRIENNE GILLESPIE • HIDDEN VILLA MAIN HOUSE • 26870 MOODY ROAD LAH • *OIL ON CANVAS* • *24" x 26"*

Built in 1929, the Duveneck's family home is now home to Hidden Villa administration staff offices and is used for meetings and social events.

JEAN STRUTHERS • HIDDEN VILLA BARN • 26870 MOODY ROAD LAH • *WATERCOLOR ON PAPER • 8" X 12"*

LARRAINE HUGHES • LOS ALTOS HILLS TOWN HALL • 26379 FREMONT ROAD • *WATERCOLOR ON PAPER* • *17" x 23"*

"Toute nationa a le gouvernement qu'lle merite." Joseph De Maistre 1811

Index of Artwork

Paint The Town Artists